ASLANT

To Emily,

Thank you so much for coming!

Apr. 2019

ASLANT

JOHN HARVEY

PHOTOGRAPHS BY
MOLLY ERNESTINE BOILING

Molly Ernestine

Shoestring Press

All rights reserved. No part of this work covered by the copyright herein may be reproduced or used in any means—graphic, electronic, or mechanical, including copying, recording, taping, or information storage and retrieval systems—without written permission of the publisher.

Printed by imprintdigital
Upton Pyne, Exeter
www.digital.imprint.co.uk

Typesetting by narrator
www.narrator.me.uk
info@narrator.me.uk
033 022 300 39

Cover design by Molly Ernestine Boiling

Published by Shoestring Press
19 Devonshire Avenue, Beeston, Nottingham, NG9 1BS
(0115) 925 1827
www.shoestringpress.co.uk

First published 2019
© Copyright: John Harvey
© Photographs copyright (including front cover): Molly Ernestine Boiling

The moral right of the author has been asserted.

ISBN 978-1-912524-09-9

for Sarah

CONTENTS

Curve	3
Voyage	5
Christmas Day	6
Bailey's Mistake (Again)	8
Epitaph	9
I Remember	17
Monk at the 5 Spot	20
Art Pepper	22
Lester Young	23
Honeymoon	31
The U.S. Botanical Gardens Washington D.C.	32
Breakwater	33
After Corot	34
Light in August	35
Notes	38

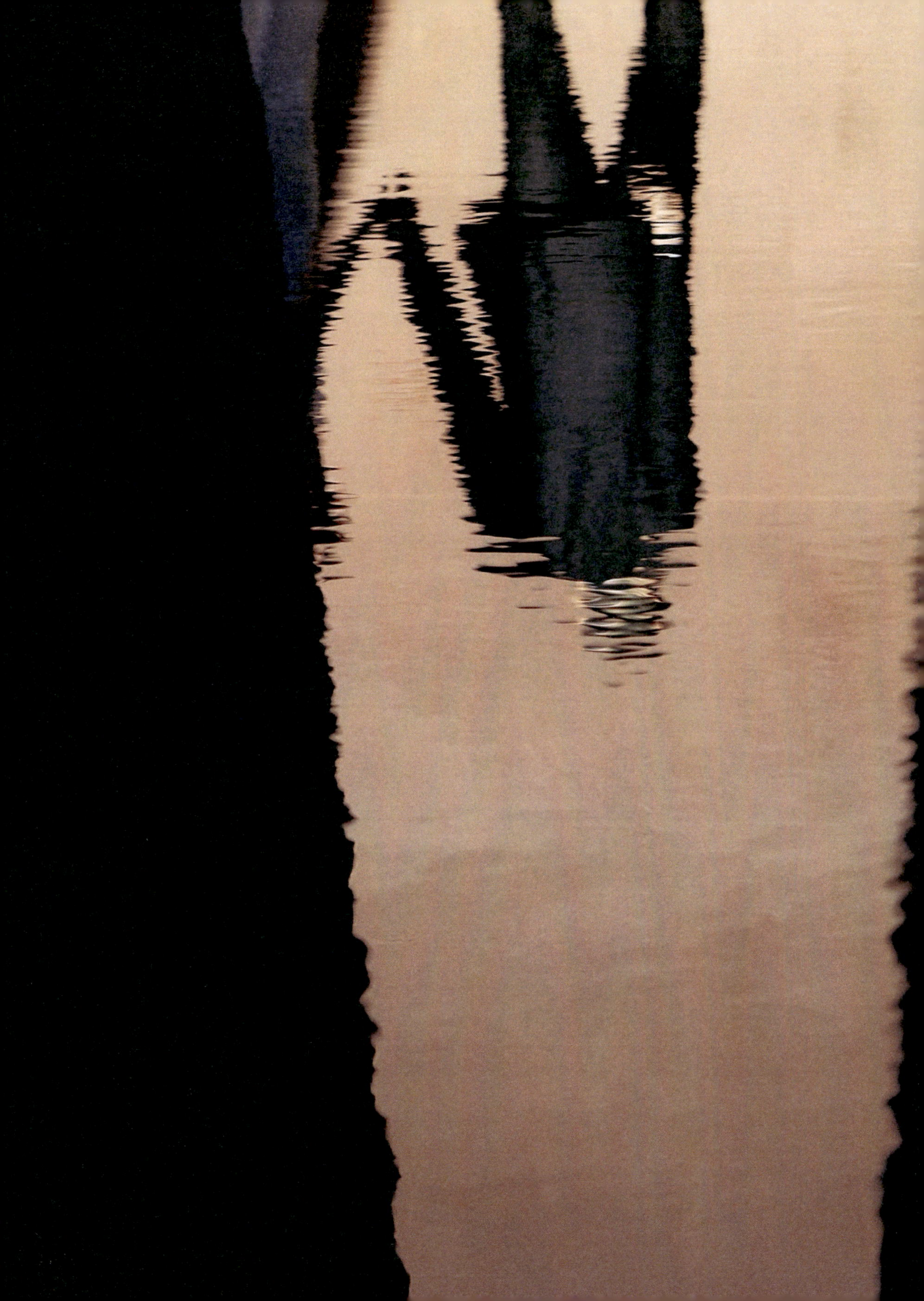

CURVE

Bridget Riley: The Curve—Paintings 1961–2014
De La Warr Pavilion, Bexhill: August, 2015

Late summer already
and the swifts that raced the canyon
of our suburban street,
criss-crossing from nest to nest,
have left swiftly as they arrived.

Our daughter is in Paris,
dreaming of becoming seventeen

Cast adrift
we catch the morning train
through fields of yellowing wheat
toward the sea;
the light oscillating
on the water's surface,
patterning across the painter's canvas,
ever moving, iridescent,
rarely what it seems.

What are you doing? you asked,
when, walking beside you, I first
threaded my fingers through yours.
Evening, it would have been, the air
about us urgent, electric,
my shoulder brushing yours.

Now the sweet heat of nights
and insatiable afternoons
has ripened into this:
the accidental touch of bodies
and flustering of hands;
the lushness of late-flowering
blackberries, their juices
sticky rich upon the skin.

Feet bare on shingle, wearing
your black dress with its green sash,
you walk cautiously to the water's edge
and stand there looking out:
the blur of motion on the horizon,
the far prospect of land;
the impossibility of leaving.

Have I ever said *I love you* and not meant it?
Yes, but not to you.

For an instant it's as if my breath has stopped:
then you turn and come back to where I'm waiting,
small shells like keepsakes tight
in the palm of your hand.

VOYAGE

They haunt us, the dead.
Not in some scary Gothic way,
the creak of footsteps on rotting board,
ragged breath corrupting the air,
but sudden and unsuspected,
like the time my friend Sue looked up
and saw her father in the audience,
clear as day, as she was listening to Mahler 9.
There then gone.

This morning walk on which we set out,
stride by stride; a ritual born of need,
the need to stretch our limbs in time, together,
father and daughter walking side by side—
much as I would have walked with my father
when he was half the age I am now.

The haze that hovers over the city—
fragments of buildings, like masts of tall ships
stalled on some outward voyage—
has faded by the time we reach the highest point
and turn to face the sun.

My mother, in the last years of her life,
would tell of my father standing quietly
at the end of the bed when she awoke,
the old sports coat, the one he counted second best,
in need still of needle and thread;
the sweet scent of tobacco from his pipe
lingering long after he had disappeared.

Where, I wonder, when the moment's passed,
the ships slipped away silent on the tide,
will I appear, unbidden, by your side?
The bench, perhaps, where we used to rest;
my shoulder, from nowhere, brushing yours,
so that you turn, surprised, a look of fear and recognition
stalling in your eyes.

CHRISTMAS DAY

Christmas morning, the sky
an opaque unhindered grey;
upstairs, our daughter,
returned for the holiday,
is in her old room, sleeping;
her mother's cough, brittle,
as she catches her breath on the stairs.

Slow-footed, careful, her grandparents
sleep on in unfamiliar rooms,
soon they will shuffle on their coats and shoes
and make their way through quiet streets
to early morning mass.

A timid boy of nine or ten,
let out of school, I hurried past
the Catholic Church on the hill,
copper dome gleaming green,
fearful lest in my haste I forgot,
as the Christian brothers ordered,
to doff my cap in respect
and brought down the wrath
of a watchful God. Remember:
He can see you everywhere.

When I was in kindergarten,
waiting in the corridor
for the teacher to arrive,
I punched Anthony Hipsley
for squirting his water pistol
at the picture of the Sacred Heart
that hung from the classroom door
and was duly admonished
and made to stand in the corner
to contemplate the error of my ways.

Last night we sat late, listening
to that motet by Vivaldi,
the one from the movie,
nulls in mundo pax sincere:
in this world there is no honest peace.

Timisoara, you called out earlier
in answer to some question
already forgotten, a game
of little consequence born of boredom,
while the news from Aleppo
plays out, silent, on the screen
behind us: street after street
of broken houses, ghosts of
Dresden, Hiroshima, Nagasaki,
Beirut, Grozny, Mosul, Palmyra … .

Give me a word for a virtue
associated with kindness,
benevolence and goodwill,
beginning with the letter H,
eight letters … .

Shadows lengthen in the hall,
Prayers rest, unspoken.

BAILEY'S MISTAKE (AGAIN)

for Sarah

Sailing out from Boston across the Gulf of Maine,
course set north by north-east and bound for Lubec,
a four-masted schooner under the command
of a Captain Bailey, cargo of lumber lashed
fast to the deck, became enmeshed in fog
as it neared the shore and somewhere short
of West Quoddy Head, beached itself astride a ridge
of land from which there was no easy redress.

When the fog cleared and they found themselves
marooned close in to a pleasant looking bay,
rather than admit he had run his ship aground
through error, Bailey ordered his crew to unload
the lumber and carry it ashore and there they built
their own homes and thrived in what came to be known
as Bailey's Mistake, happy in their accidental lives.

So it was, my love, some twenty years ago or more,
that I stumbled blindly, more than a little battered,
discarded, bemused, into the safety of your arms.
That Bailey, he knew how to learn from his mistakes,
let them lift away on the tide while you strike out
for firmer land and once sure you're home,
sink roots and stay.

EPITAPH

December morning, the sky a faint pellucid grey
and I'm reading Robert Hass's poem about his brother,
the one where he remembers Mississippi John Hurt's
song about the death of Louis Collins; the brother
who could only think about Billie Holiday
when he should have been thinking about
what he was going to do now he'd been evicted
from his apartment because he couldn't pay
the rent, and worse, much worse … .

Angels laid him away
Laid him six feet under the clay

Life, they say, is a litany of dying.

My friend, Angus, with whom I wrote
more than a dozen westerns with titles like
Death and Jack Shade and *Dead Man's Hand*,
died in his bed, alone; mercifully overcome
by fumes when the cigarette he'd fallen
asleep smoking sparked the sheets to flame.

The police, when they came, alarmed
at the discovery of a Colt .45 in a drawer
and fearing there might be more, a cache
of arms perhaps, cordoned off the street
until the weapon was declared a replica and safe.
He would have liked that, Angus, had he known.
Snug in his bed now in the shade of Sherwood
Forest where we saw him laid to rest.

Two or three years, the oncology doctor said
when we asked him the best prognosis—
not the consultant but one of her team—
young, his accent uncertain, Spanish perhaps,
a mark like a birth mark, high on his cheek.
Beside me, I felt you tense and heard
the sharp intake of breath when I asked again
and the answer was the same.

Perhaps I'm making up the detail of the birth mark,
but, then again, perhaps not.

Nothing left to do but shake hands, stand and leave.
Outside, we turn toward each other and the words
catch in my throat like the buttons on a child's coat,
fingers fumbling awkwardly, struggling to be free.

I heard from our daughter today, happy in Australia,
Melbourne; happier, I think, more fulfilled
than she's ever been. Soon, despite herself perhaps,
she will come home. A while, at least.

I close the book and think a little, also, about Billie Holiday,
her voice at the end, ravaged almost past care;
the jauntiness of Mississippi John Hurt's guitar,
offsetting the finality of his words.
We all earn an epitaph, spoken or not.
What was it Auden said? Stop all the clocks.
I'd be content. I think, if for just long enough
to let the coffin past, they cordoned off the streets.

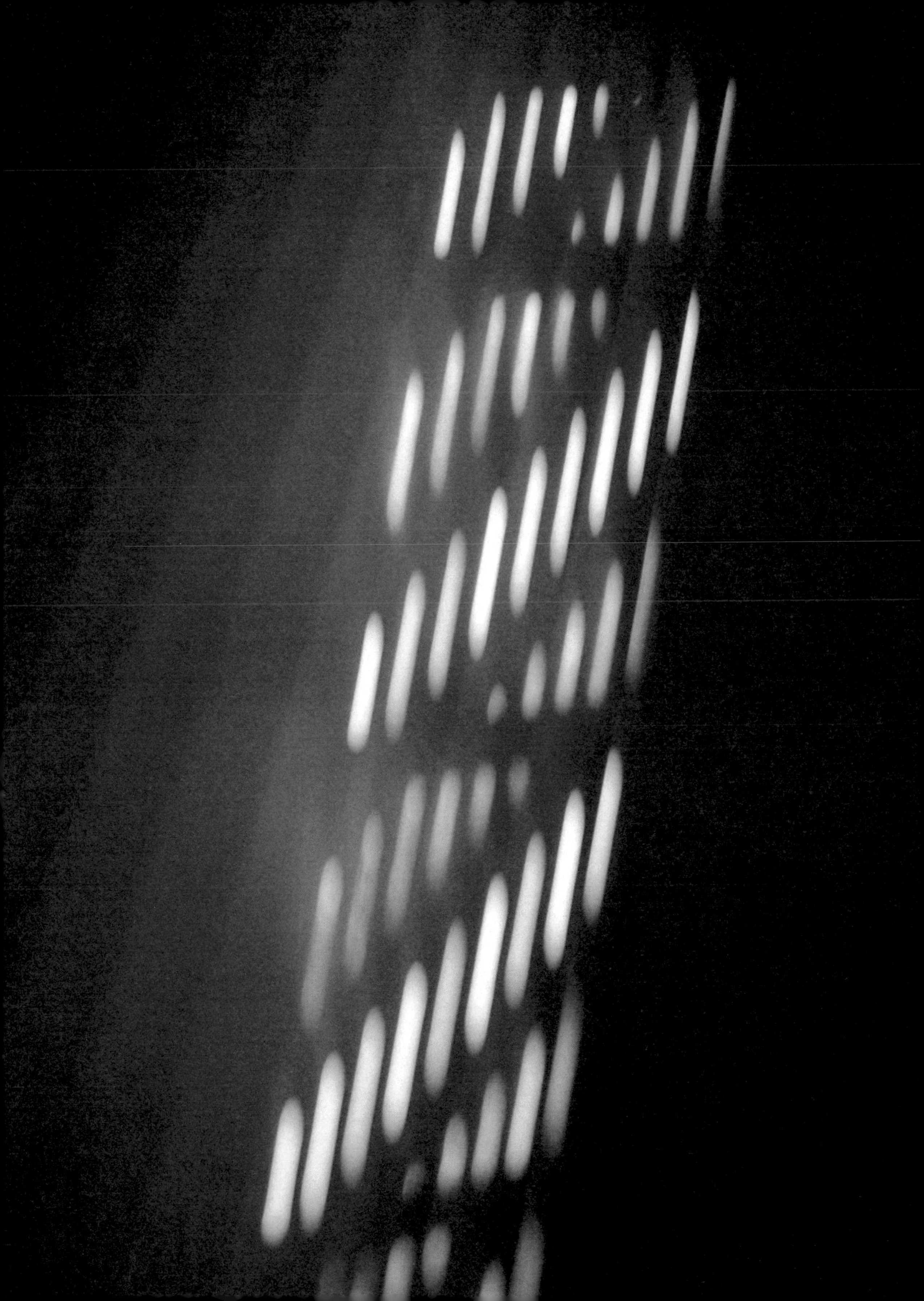

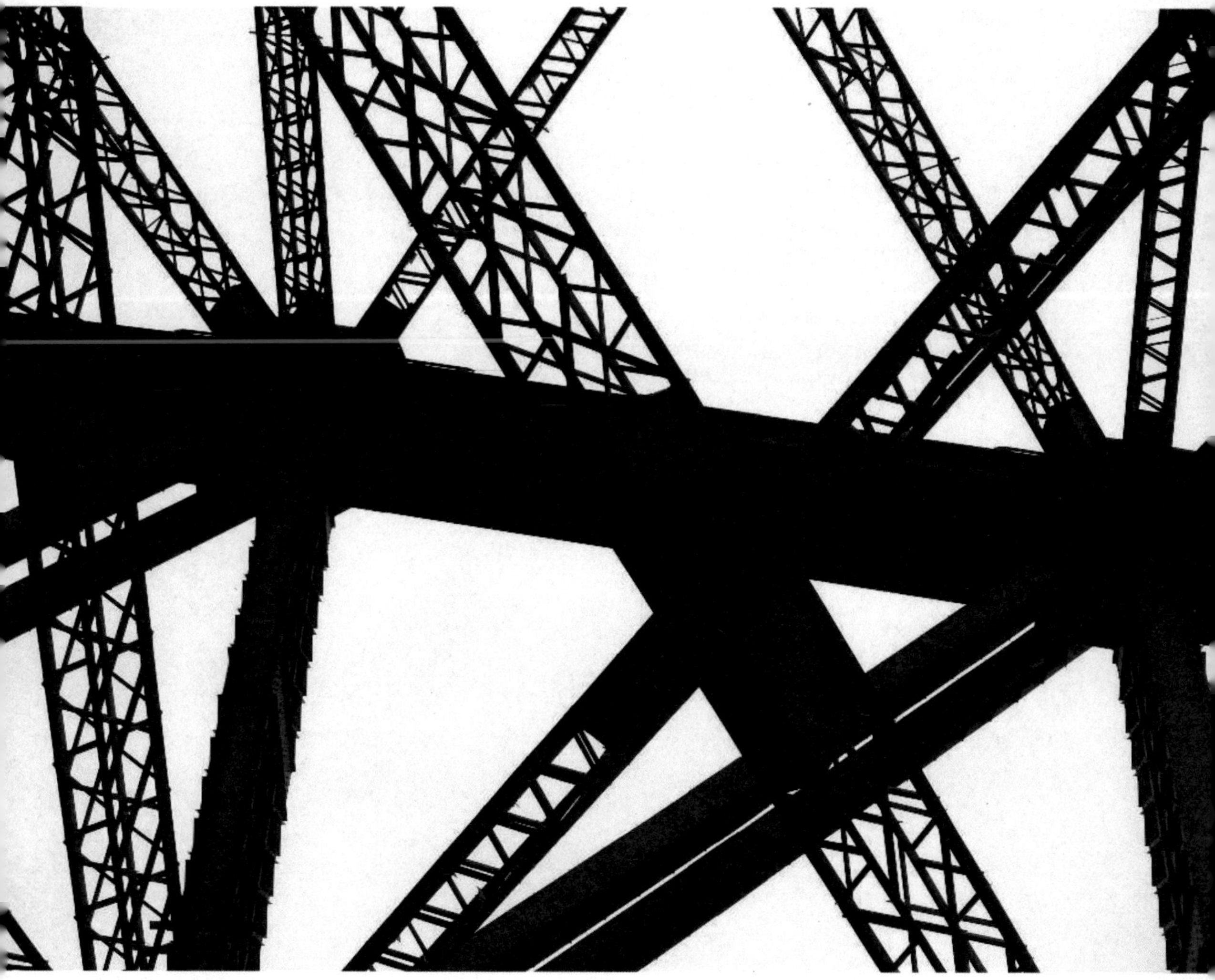

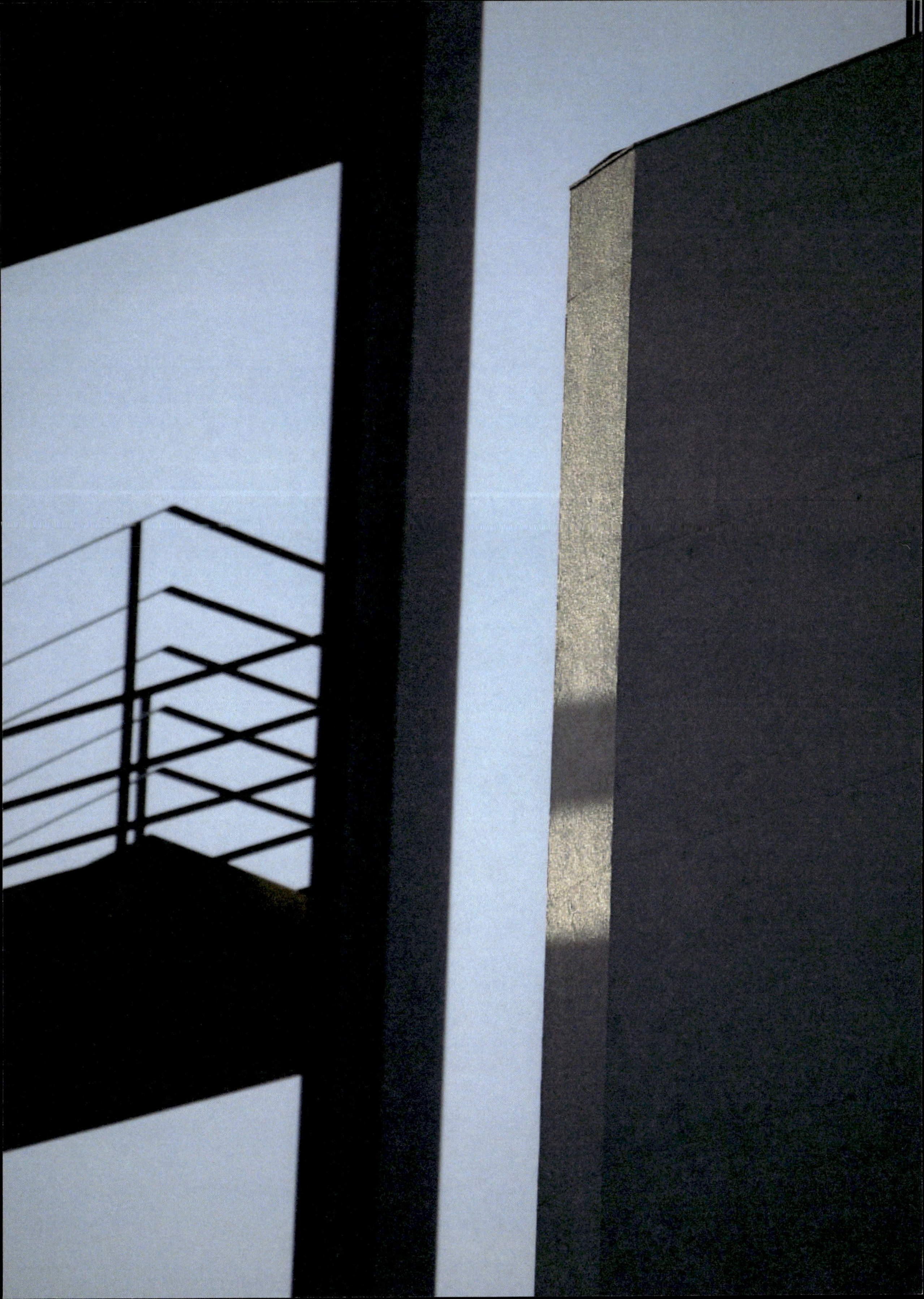

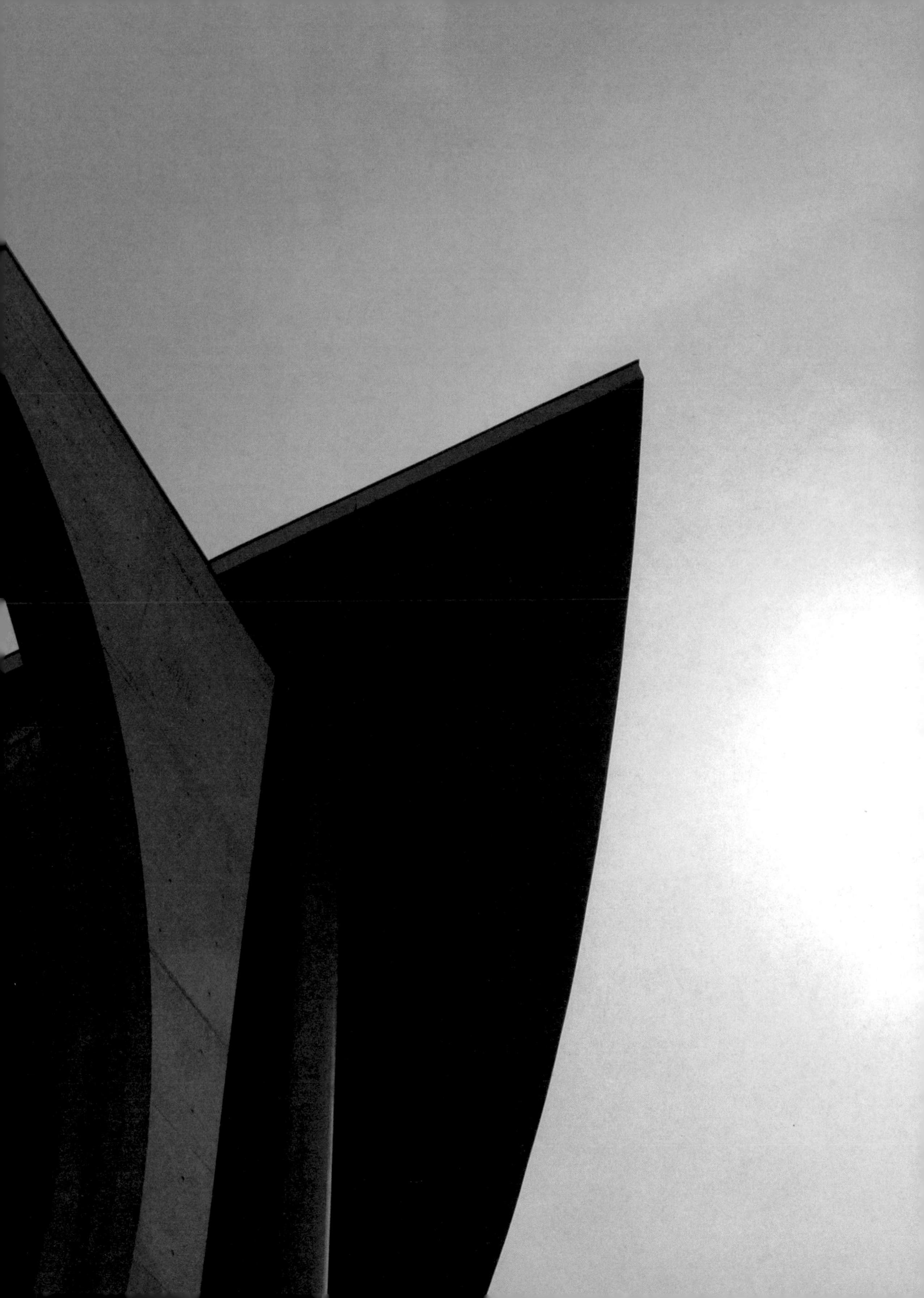

I REMEMBER

I remember the first time I heard a big band
or any kind of jazz at all—
sitting across from my mother and aunt
in the splendour of Lyons Corner House
at Marble Arch, feasting on cakes and petit fours
from a glass cake stand tiered like a chandelier
and listening in muted amazement
to Ivy Benson & Her All-Girl Orchestra
swinging their way gloriously
through the fusty afternoon.

Before that, I suppose it had been my father,
in the room we liked to call the lounge,
tapping his wedding ring finger
on the silver surface of his cigarette lighter
in time to Winifred Atwell's *Britannia Rag*,
Fats Waller's *Alligator Crawl*.

And then, a little older,
parties at my friend Michael's house,
where his Uncle Mac, six foot and sixteen stone,
would get himself up in women's clothes—
skirt, rouched blouse with false boobs,
stockings, suspenders, bright red lipstick and rouge,
and, between jokes I didn't always understand,
impersonate Sophie Tucker singing *Some of These Days*
and, a family favourite, *Nobody Loves a Fat Girl,
But Oh How a Fat Girl Can Love*.

Cabaret over, we'd sneak into the room
which housed the wind-up gramophone
and rummage through the piles of 78s,
bypassing Doris Day and Frankie Laine
until we found the Mills Brothers' version
of Tommy Dorsey's *Opus One*
or *Pennies from Heaven* by Teddy Wilson
and his Orchestra with Billie Holiday, 'vocal refrain'.

Once a month on Sunday afternoons,
setting homework aside, I'd catch the bus
to Oxford Circus, Argyle Street,

Ted Heath Swing Sessions at the London Palladium,
sitting in the front row of the balcony—
fifteen, I'd be, sixteen at most
thrilling to the sound of *Bakerloo Non-Stop*,
The Champ, *Blues for Moderns*.
Ronnie Verrell's drums propelling *Hawaiian War Chant*
to the point of near hysteria and beyond.

Then, in 1956, unbelievably,
Louis Armstrong in London with the All Stars—
Ed Hall on clarinet, Barrett Deems, Trummy Young.
Louis up there on the revolving stage at the Empress Hall,
a one-legged dancer called Peg-Leg Bates
his warm-up act, as if he were some kind
of vaudeville performer … But what music!
The gravelled out sound of his voice,
the high notes of his trumpet,
imperious and clear, soaring
so magnificently over everything.

Seventeen, eighteen were my trad jazz years,
bands with banjos and fancy waistcoats,
silly names; fine musicians, none the less,
in among the glitter and the dross,
the countless times the *Saints* went marching in—
Archie Semple, Bruce Turner, Al Gay—
Sandy Brown, who played clarinet like no other
and sang the blues in rasping tones
that stretched from Edinburgh
to the Mississippi Delta and back again.

Sunday nights we'd go,
a bunch of us from grammar school,
off to the Fishmongers' Arms at Wood Green,
down pints of bitter and jive,
sometimes, emboldened, taking two girls at a time,
to the brash Chicago-style Dixieland
of the Alex Welsh Band,
waiting for the chance to holler *Ooo-Yah, Ooo-Yah*
in unison with Lennie Hastings
when, at the end of his second or third four bar break,
he would throw his drumsticks in the air and shout,
catching them as they rebounded off his snare.

I saw him later, Alex,
Nottingham Rhythm Club, one of his last gigs ever,
sick, barely playing, a chorus at best;
midway through the second set
he brought up a gout of phlegm,
lethal, black as coal, face torn
between embarrassment and pain:
a few weeks later he was dead.
So much music to remember:
George Melly hamming his way
through *Frankie and Johnny*;
Humph's eight-piece band riffing
mightily behind Jimmy Rushing;
all-nighters at the Flamingo—
Georgie Fame and the Blue Flames,
Zoot Money and his Big Roll Band.
Crombies, be-bop, rolled collars, Cecil Gee's;
the original Ronnie Scott's
in a basement on Gerard Street,
cool nights at Studio 51, the Marquee.
Tubby Hayes walking, unannounced,
on stage at the Festival Hall
to take the empty chair in Ellington's
saxophone section—a rare moment
of patriotic pride welling up inside.

In Nottingham also, the great Ben Webster
slumped on a stool at the Dancing Slipper,
too drunk to bring tenor to his lips,
yet stubbornly refusing to leave the stage
until Bill Kinnell, with reluctance,
had him bodily lifted down
so the evening could continue.
Which is the thing, I suppose;
no matter who, no matter what,
the music, the jazz, in whatever guise,
whoever's hands, plays on.

MONK AT THE 5 SPOT

They've all been here to see him: Ginsburg,
who would read here himself on a Monday
night, the musicians' night off; Mailer, too,
sitting, as he said, just five feet away from
Monk's hands on the keyboard. Hands that
jabbed down flat upon the keys, striking two
notes at once, seeking out the spaces in between.

But tonight it's Larry Rivers and his crowd,
jammed together round a table at the back;
Frank O'Hara in earnest conversation
with Grace Hartigan, while Rivers,
a musician himself, bends one ear to what's
being said, the other angled toward the stand,
where Monk, dark glasses shielding his eyes,
is starting to rock back and forth on the piano stool,
elbows angled out, fingers feeling for a rhythm
in the bottom hand, while the right finds angles of its own,
his foot jabbing down, punctuating the broken line,
as the drummer, seated at Monk's back,
follows each new shift and shuffle,
quick and careful as a hawk, and the bassist,
eyes closed, feels for an underlying pulse.

And all this time, head down, horn hooked
over his shoulder, John Coltrane waits, biding his time ...

*Blue Monk, 'Round Midnight,
Epistrophy; Ruby, My Dear.*

O'Hara has just said something that has made
Hartigan laugh aloud, hand flying to her mouth,
and as Helen Frankenthaler leans across the table
to catch what was said, Rivers rolls his eyes and sighs.

Sometimes, when Coltrane solos,
Monk sits at the piano, hands hanging down
as if in some state of trance; at others, unbidden,
he will rise up and, arms akimbo, stirred
by something he alone hears in Trane's playing,
something reminding him of childhood, perhaps,
perform some slow and antic dance.

But tonight he has remained perfectly still,
contributing the occasional chord, and now,
as Coltrane leans back into the applause,
Monk launches himself, without warning,
into a jinking solo which skips and leans
and finally builds into an angular arpeggio
which calls to mind a man stumbling headlong
down a flight of stairs, never quite losing his balance,
not falling but saving himself with an upward swoop
and final double-handed chord, so sudden,
so emphatic, that the crowd, almost as one,
catches its breath and even Frank O'Hara
is stunned into silence.

I Mean You. The 5 Spot, September, 1957.

ART PEPPER

New York, 1972.
The Village Vanguard, Thursday night,
the first of three.

A steady pulse from bass and drums:
the pianist feeds him eight bars
then eight more and then sixteen
and still he stands, immobile,
alto cradled in his hands,
while in front of him
faces swim and blur
and the conversation swells

Coke, heroin, methadone,
a gallon of cheap wine a day,
spleen ruptured and removed.
prison brought him night sweats,
pain, purged him of everything
but this ... .

The reed like burnt rubber
in his mouth, notes catch fire,
burn and scatter
like cinders underfoot

As long as he can play
he lives ...

LESTER YOUNG

They called him fey, a mama's boy,
apologetic, shy; mumbling a made-up
language all his own; rolled their eyes
at the way he held his horn, angled off
to one side instead of thrusting forward
toward the crowd, the microphone.

When he first went on the road with Fletcher Henderson,
Henderson's wife, Leora, shut him in the closet
with recordings of the man he'd been called in to replace,
made him listen again and again to that raw-edged,
muscular sound. All belly, as Lester liked to say
dismissively. Belly out.

It wasn't till he was with Basie they really started to listen,
stepping out from the section to solo on *Dickie's Dream*
and *Jive at Five*; *Jumpin' at the the Woodside*, *Lester Leaps In*.
A succession, often, of single notes
that built and built until suddenly, irrevocably,
like spray striking the shore, they broke
into a pattern that was his and his alone,
witty, intelligent and strong. Supple yet lean.

One night in Watts, a fan, resplendent
in zoot suit and chain, invited Lester
and some of the others to be his guest
after hours at the bar. Many gins later he took
Lester to one side and showed him his badge:
the Draft Board office on 8th Street,
they'll be expecting you, 9.00 am sharp.

Private 39729502, he was sent for training at Fort Arthur,
served much of his time in the stockade,
locked in a world of his own for disobeying orders
he did not properly understand. When finally
they discharged him as unfit, unfit was what he was.

He took barbiturates, drank gin, anything
to dull the pain slowly rupturing inside.
Played dinner lounges, one-roomed bars
and supper clubs from Oklahoma to D.C.
Toured Europe with Jazz at the Phil.
But now he is tired, wants to lie down,
the pains in his stomach crucifying,
but no, "You doin' great, man! You fine!"

At the Blue Note in Paris, face bloated,
short of breath, body shrivelled and thin,
each wavering note, its sound all but lost
amid the desultory conversation, might be his last.
As his thought unravels his fingers slip away.
On the plane back to New York, the veins
leading to his oesophagus have started to burst
and he is vomiting blood. Less than a day later,
in an upstairs room at the Alvin Hotel,
high over Broadway, riven with pain,
he lies down on an unmade bed
and closes his eyes one final time.
Lester Willis Young: August, 1909–March, 1959.

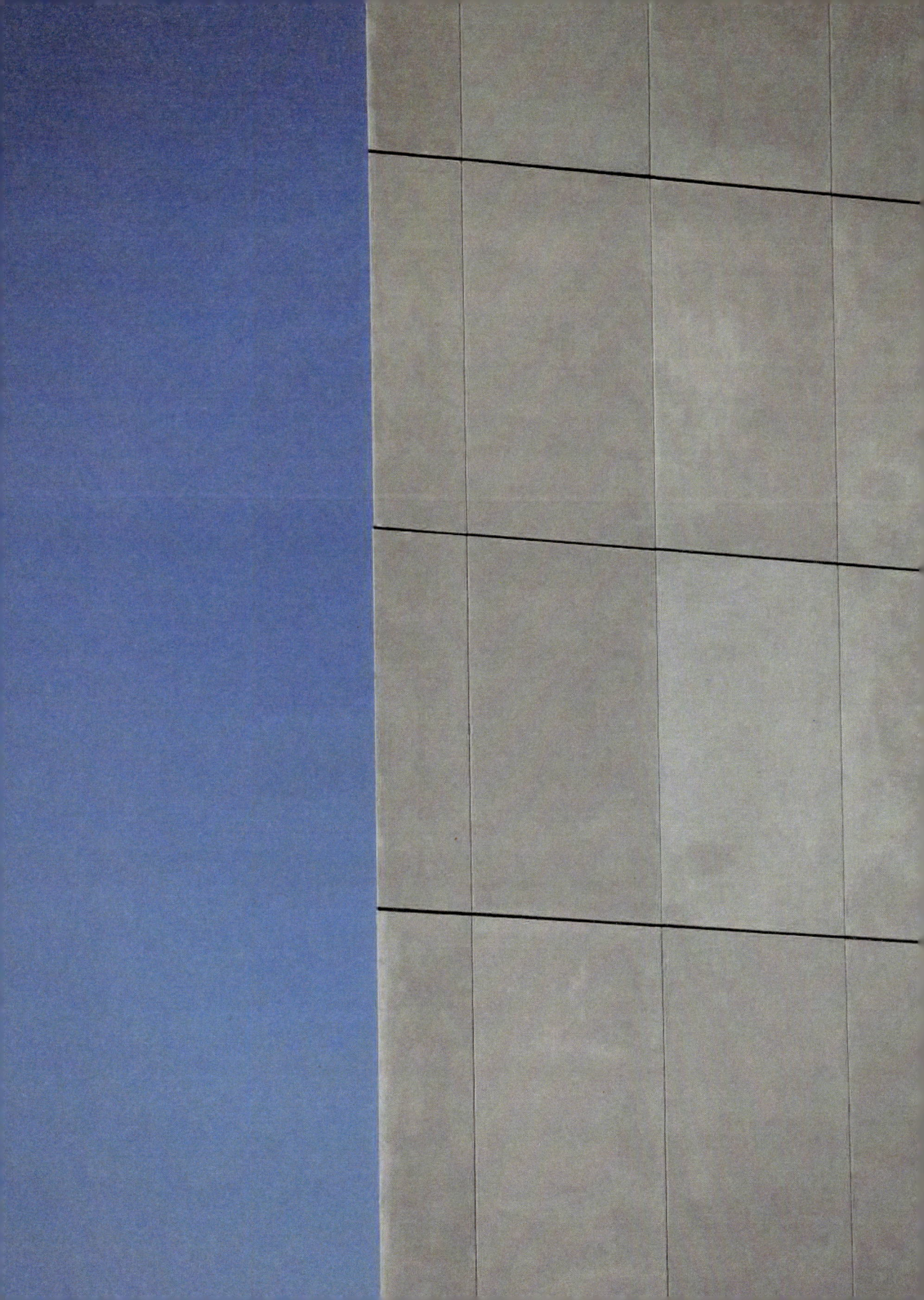

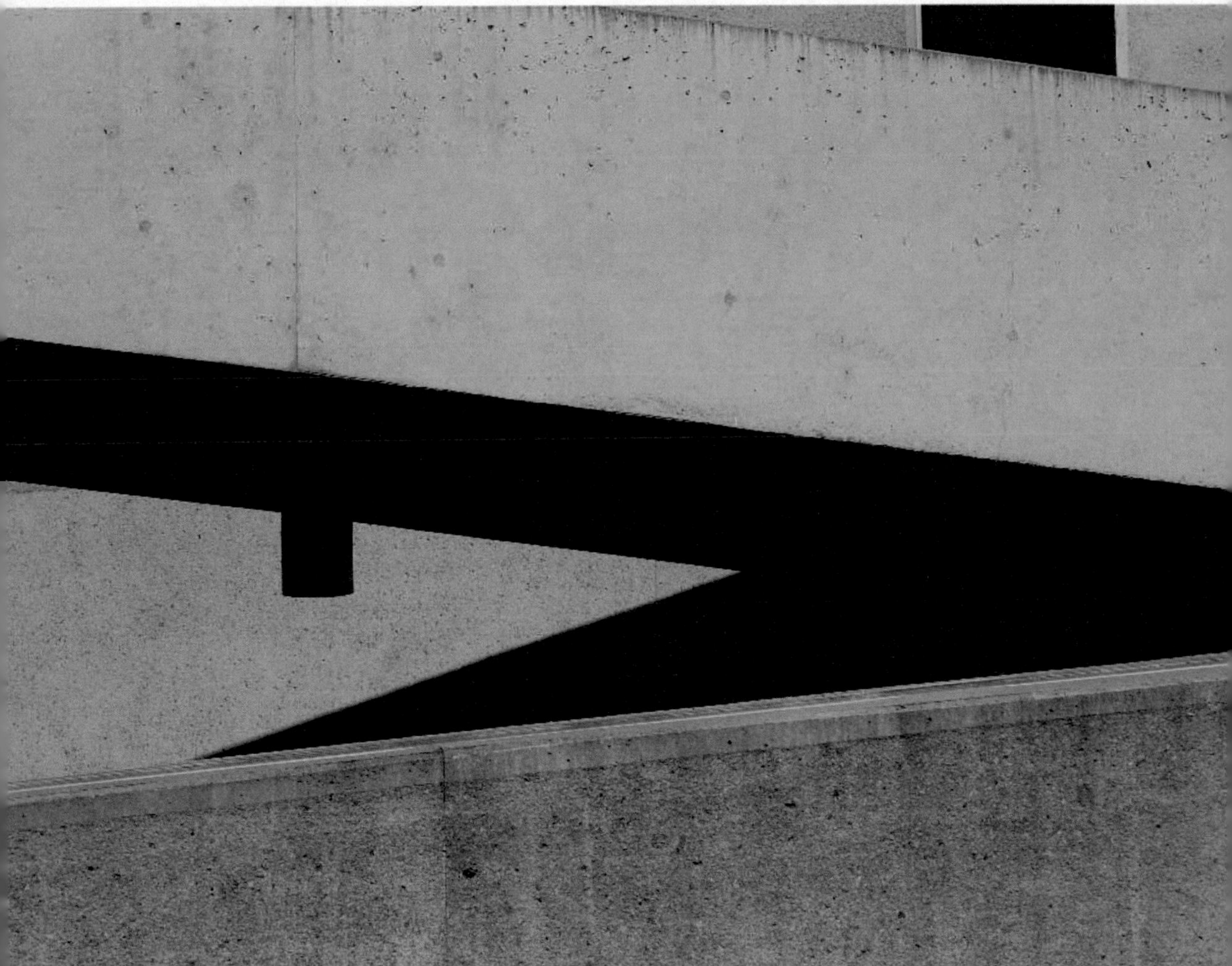

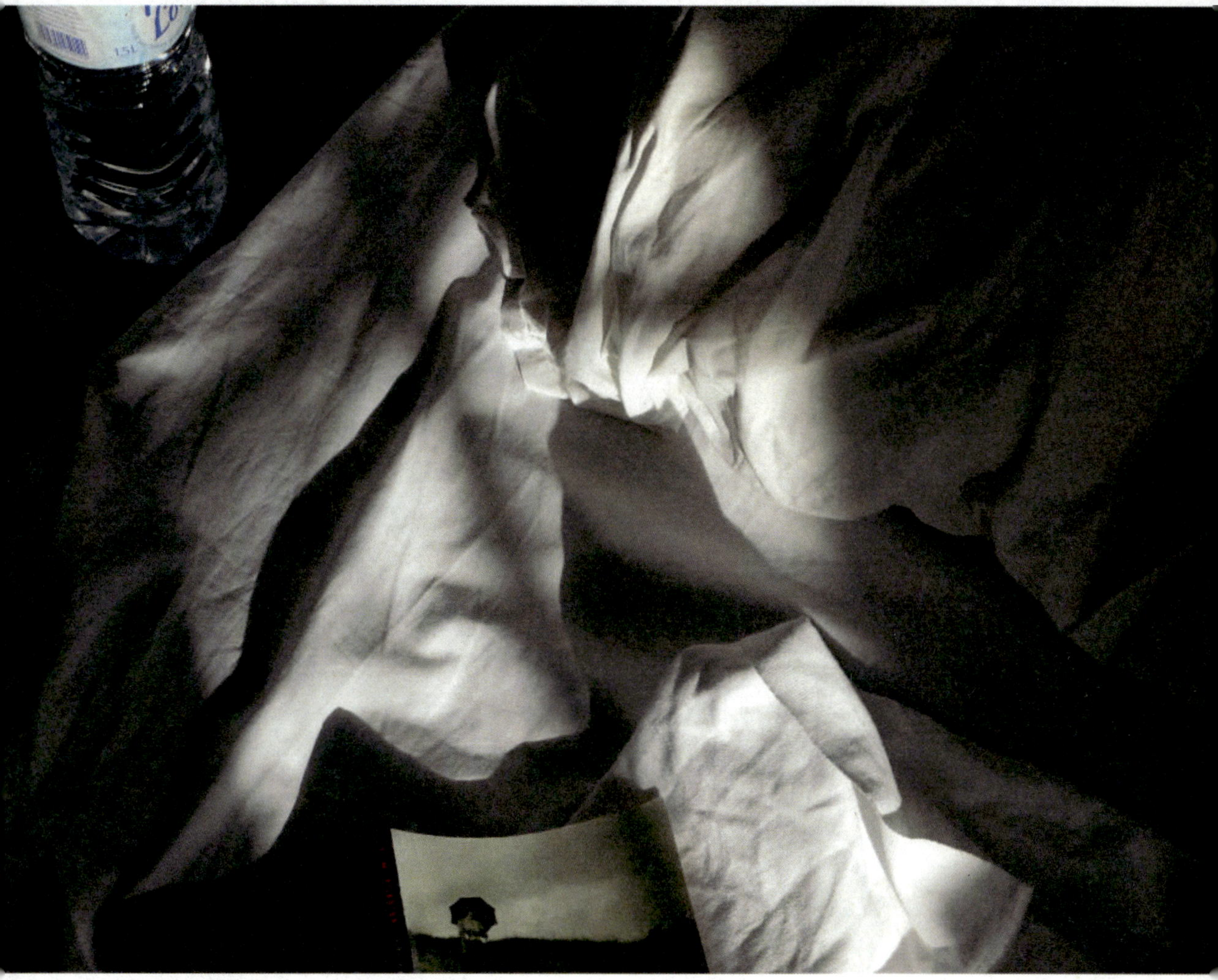

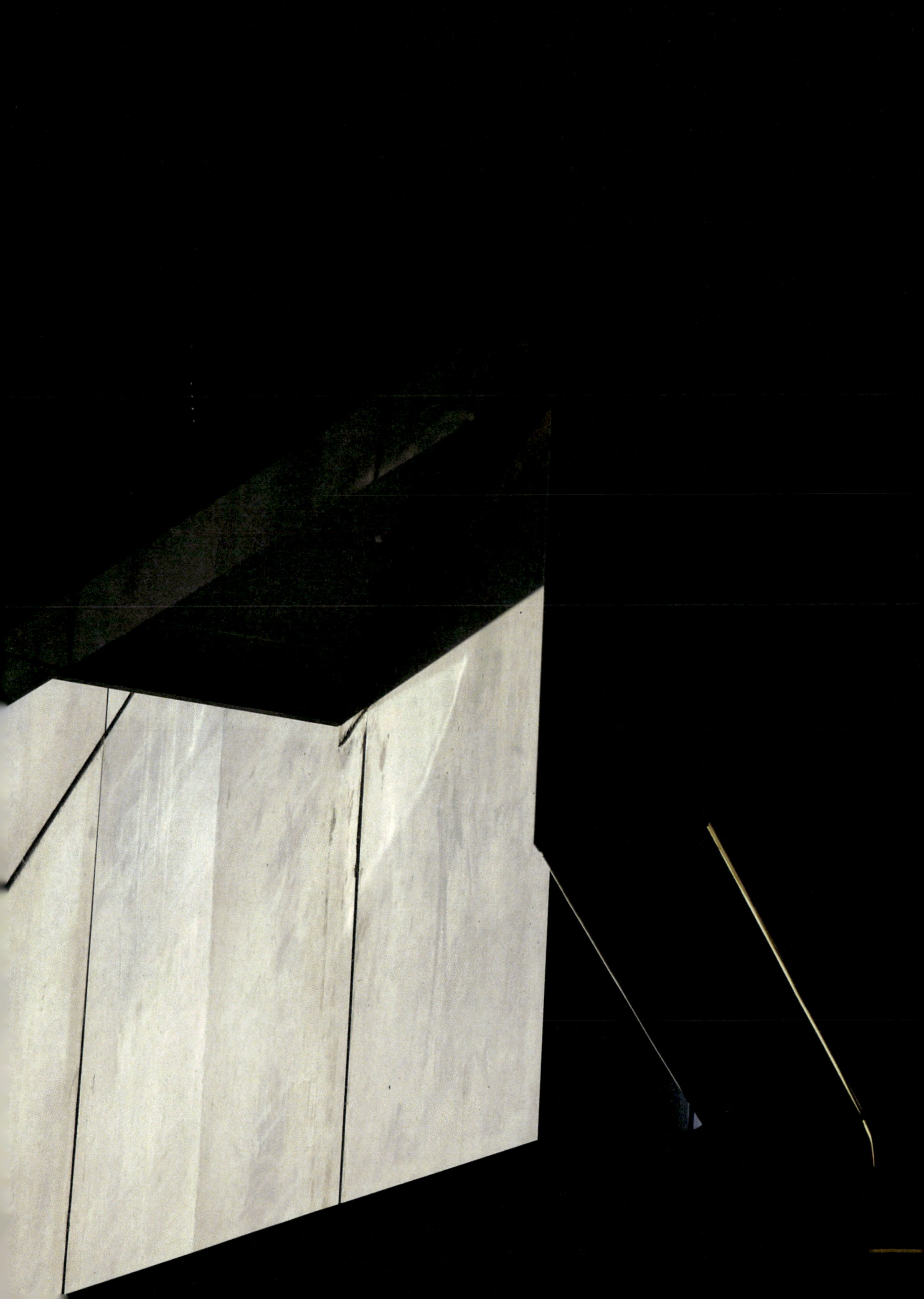

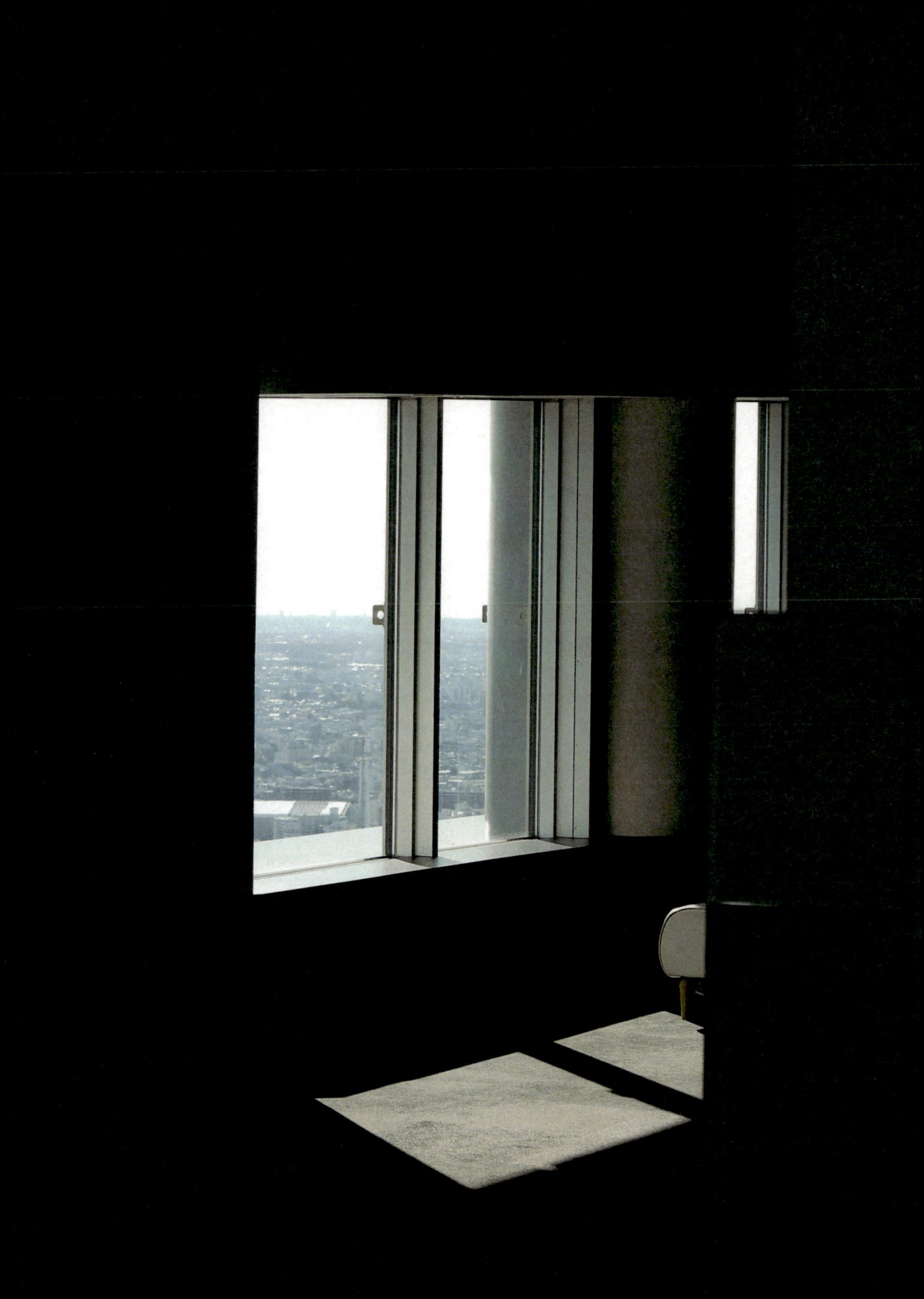

HONEYMOON

The swimsuit he'd been wearing earlier,
my father, a single strap draped,
Johnny Weissmuller style, over one shoulder,
set aside now in favour of pale slacks,
white shirt, collar splayed open
across the lapels of his blazer;
sitting a little self-consciously
alongside my mother, smart
in her polka-dot dress, white shoes;
the two of them staring back at the camera,
that picture the beach photographer
will display proudly later in his window.

The first time he'd set eyes on my mother,
she'd been standing close against the piano,
her voice small and clear
yet somehow distant, disarming;
the way, as the last notes faded,
silence seemed to fold about her …

Now she sits with her arm resting
on the check tablecloth, her hand
close to his but not quite touching;
the café doors behind them open,
waiter hovering, a tune somewhere playing.
the world waiting,

Those carefree days before the war:
Ostend, Spring 1939

THE U.S. BOTANICAL GARDENS WASHINGTON D.C.

The floor is azure blue tile
slick with the residue
of that morning's watering,
green hose resting
slack between the leaves.

We would come here, safe,
afternoons, and sit, not touching,
humidity in the 90s
and helicopters hovering
a block beyond the Hill.

Though you are here no longer
I reach out to touch your arm,
trace the sweat, the way it beads
around the curve of your skin

From the display of medicinal
herbs, I break small leaves
into the palm of my hand:
yarrow, for internal bleeding,
foxglove for the muscles of the heart.

And when we meet, a year
from now, by chance, the
departure lounge at Heathrow,
the platform at Gare du Nord,
that harbour front café, and,
uncertain whether or not to kiss me,
you hold out, instead, your hand,
I will slip into it these remedies
I have long carried, in the knowledge
that, nurtured, love flowers in the darkest place.

BREAKWATER

She woke, that summer, each day
at four twenty-five precisely;
lay there waiting for the first birds,
their anxious call,
the dawn pearling off the sea.

The last card he'd sent her:
Having a grand time, Mam,
wish you were here.

She can hear his voice, low
among the day's meanderings,
the shuffle of the busy shoreline,
back and forth against the tide.

Today, she'll clear out that cupboard,
herbs and spices she'd read about
in some forgotten recipe and never used;
jars to be emptied, washed, re-stored;
shelves scrubbed clean
within an inch of their lives.

You damned fool, his father had said,
the first time he saw his son in uniform.

She'd moved here not long after the funeral:
a walk along the pier after supper,
a cup of something warm, a few pages
of her book before putting out the light.

Tomorrow, perhaps, she'll take the bus
north along the coast, watch the waves
battering the breakwater at Staithes,
gulls wheeling past the cliff face
into the wind.

AFTER COROT

'After Corot' 1979–1982, Howard Hodgkin

the train turning into the bay
enough to bring tears to the eyes

sleeping, your skin ivory,
the reach and fall of your breathing

    your hand

in the painting everything
at a distance
cliff, harbour, sky, sea

tight within a frame
within a frame

only wait
the light breaks white
on the horizon
mastheads etch contours
beyond the wall's bulk

as a small boat painted red
hoves into view
the land slips
another foot toward the sea

    you throw up your arm

untrammelled
blue seeps beneath the edges
of the frame

the rocking of the train
as it rounds the curve

    your waking breath

the sea

LIGHT IN AUGUST

By late summer the rockets no longer fall in pairs
    but randomly,
like sunspots across the eyes

The last convoys lie beyond the walls,
    abandoned;
most aid now comes indifferently from the sky

In the centre of some other city
she is crouched down, reading,
eyes shielded from the sun

He can hear the page buckle
against her finger as she turns;
the faintest trace of sweat,
salt like olives, on her skin

Just yesterday a family he had known
was killed crossing the street to prayers;
meanings ascribed to love or children
no longer apply

Ignoring curfew
he walks out into the heat of day

If she turned her head aside,
he wonders would she see him
imprinted behind her eyes

She turns the page again,
    pauses
and reads on

By now, she could be anywhere
under the sun

NOTES

Monk at the 5 Spot borrows from Chapter 13 of *In a True Light* (William Heinemann, 2001).

Lester Young leans (at an angle, of course) on *Sometimes I'm Happy*, first published in *Bluer Than This* (Smith/Doorstop, 1998)

The US Botanical Gardens, Washington DC and *After Corot* first appeared, in a slightly different form, in *Bluer Than This* (Smith/Doorstop, 1998)

Light in August first appeared in a different form in *Ghosts of a Chance* (Smith/Doorstop, 1992)

Art Pepper first appeared in *Minor Key* (Five Leaves, 2009)